CC | MB | £6.50
8/2/90

History in Evidence

PREHISTORIC BRITAIN

Barry M. Marsden

Wayland

History in Evidence

Medieval Britain

Norman Britain

Prehistoric Britain

Roman Britian

Saxon Britain

Tudor Britain

Victorian Britain

Viking Britain

Cover design: Alison Anholt-White
Series design: Helen White
Consultant: Dr Margaret L Faull

Cover pictures: The main picture is Stonehenge, in
Wiltshire. The inset is a Neolithic pottery food vessel
which was found at Mildenhall, in Suffolk.

First published in 1989 by
Wayland (Publishers) Limited
61 Western Road, Hove
East Sussex BN3 1JD, England

British Library Cataloguing in Publication Data
Marsden, Barry
   Prehistoric Britain. – (History in evidence)
   1. Great Britain, to 1066
   I. Title II. Series
   941.01

   ISBN 1-85210-576-3

Edited and typeset by Kudos, Hove, East Sussex
Printed in Italy by G. Canale & C.S.p.A., Turin
Bound in France by A.G.M.

Picture acknowledgements
The publishers wish to thank the following for
permission to reproduce the illustrations on the pages
mentioned: Janet & Colin Bord *cover* (main picture), 13
(both), 19 (both), 23 (upper); Butser Ancient Farm
Project Trust, Queen Elizabeth Country Park 28, 29
(lower); Chapel Studios Picture Library 20 (lower); C M
Dixon 6 (upper), 14, 18; English Heritage 11 (lower), 20
(upper); Michael Holford *cover* (inset), 9 (lower), 11
(upper); Kudos 15; Royal Museum of Scotland 17 (both);
Skyscan 12, 15, 21, 25, 26; TOPHAM 29 (top); Trustees of
the British Museum 5 (both: Natural History Museum), 6
(lower), 7 (both), 8, 9 (upper), 10, 16, 23 (left), 27 (both).
The artwork was supplied by Malcolm S Walker 4, 11,
22, 24.

Contents

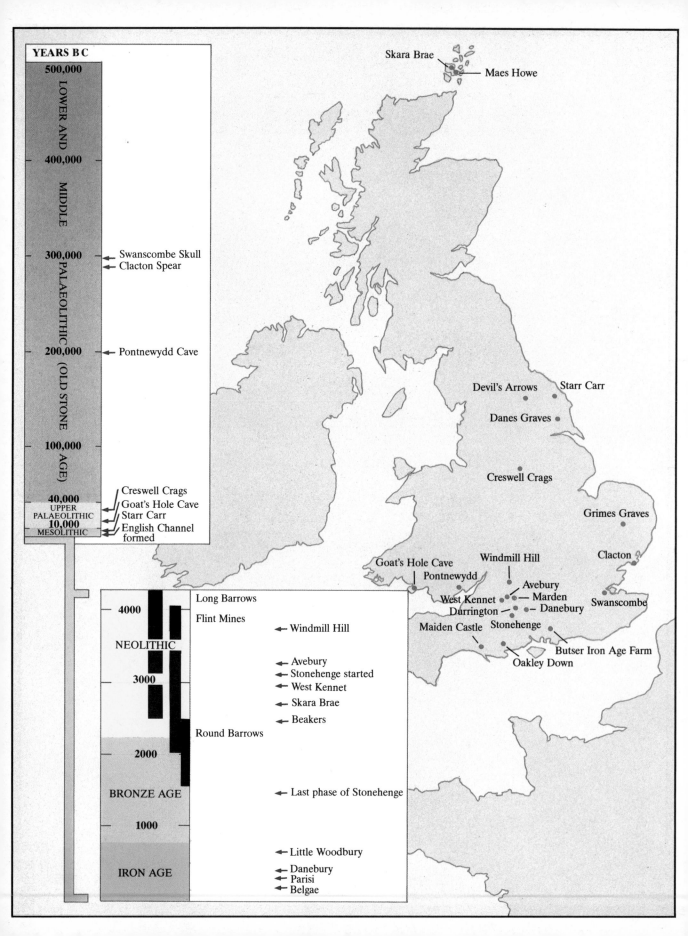

YEARS B C

500,000

LOWER AND MIDDLE PALAEOLITHIC (OLD STONE AGE)

400,000

300,000 — ← Swanscombe Skull
          ← Clacton Spear

200,000 — ← Pontnewydd Cave

100,000

40,000 — ← Creswell Crags
UPPER   ← Goat's Hole Cave
PALAEOLITHIC ← Starr Carr
10,000 — ← English Channel
MESOLITHIC   formed

4000 Long Barrows
      Flint Mines
NEOLITHIC   ← Windmill Hill

3000   ← Avebury
                             ← Stonehenge started
                             ← West Kennet
                             ← Skara Brae
                             ← Beakers
      Round Barrows

2000

BRONZE AGE   ← Last phase of Stonehenge

1000

                             ← Little Woodbury
IRON AGE
                             ← Danebury
                             ← Parisi
                             ← Belgae

Skara Brae
Maes Howe

Devil's Arrows   Starr Carr
        Danes Graves

Creswell Crags

                        Grimes Graves

                                    Clacton
Goat's Hole Cave   Windmill Hill
         Pontnewydd
                        Avebury
West Kennet   — Marden
Durrington   — Danebury   Swanscombe
Maiden Castle   Stonehenge
                        Butser Iron Age Farm
        Oakley Down

The first Britons

By 'prehistoric' we mean the time before people started writing about what was going on in their world. Groups of people appeared in Britain perhaps as long ago as 500,000 BC, during the warm periods which separated the cold times we know as the Ice Ages. They came in search of food and hunted mammoths, woolly rhinoceroses, reindeer and elephants.

At that time Britain was not an island, so the people were able to roam across Europe, looking for food and skins and furs for clothing. These early humans lived in small family groups, next to water or in caves. They rarely stayed in one place for long. Only their tools, made from stone and bone, survive. The most common stone tool was a pointed, pear-

ABOVE This is a piece of a woman's skull from 300,000 BC. It was found at Swanscombe, in Kent.

OPPOSITE This map shows all the places mentioned in this book, as well as date charts.

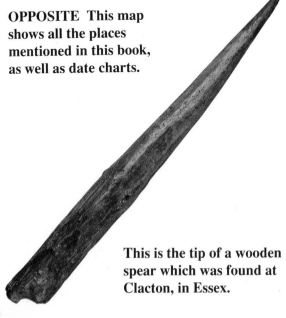

This is the tip of a wooden spear which was found at Clacton, in Essex.

shaped hand-axe. This was made by striking flakes from a lump of flint so that a point was formed. The pointed lump was then used as a tool. These hand-axes could be used to kill animals, to cut leather and meat, to carve wood and to dig up roots.

Few human remains are found from this time. Part of a woman's skull was unearthed in a gravel pit at Swanscombe, in Kent. It has been dated to 300,000 BC. Other bones, discovered in Pontnewydd Cave, north Wales, are probably 200,000 years old. One of the most interesting discoveries was a pointed wooden spear which had been preserved in peat at Clacton, in Essex. It is probably more than 300,000 years old.

The last Ice Age

Human beings, similar to what we look like today, arrived in Britain around 40,000 BC, during the last Ice Age. They belong to a race known as *Homo sapiens*, and they were more clever than the earlier hunters. They made many types of tools and weapons from stones, bones, antlers and wood. They used skins and furs for clothing. They made fires to keep warm and to cook their food. Their homes were caves, or huts made of animal skins and branches. They wore necklaces made of shells, bones and animals' teeth. They

ABOVE The entrance to a cave near Settle, West Yorkshire, which was the home of a family in the last Ice Age.

This horse's head was carved on an animal's bone. It was found in a cave at Creswell Crags, north Derbyshire.

hunted woolly rhinoceroses, elks, mammoths, cave bears and hyenas. Using all their skills and tools, they were able to survive the long, icy winters.

Several homes of these hunters have been found. At Goat's Hole Cave, Paviland, in South Wales, a young man had been buried in the cave's floor. This shows that these people believed in some kind of religious worship. The body had been

6

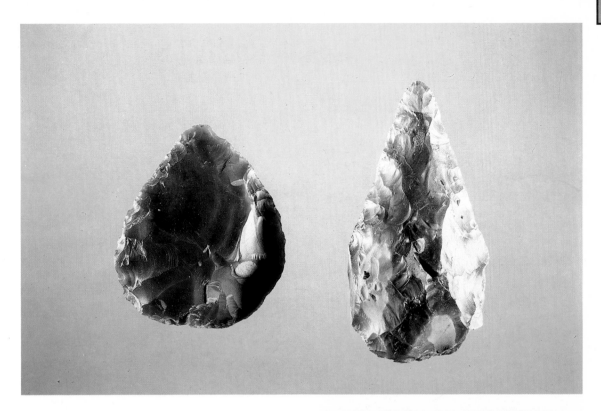

ABOVE Two flint hand-axes.

RIGHT This piece of carved antler, from Creswell Crags, perhaps once hung from a woman's neck on a leather cord.

smeared with a red powder, called ochre, perhaps as decoration. At Creswell Crags, in north Derbyshire, there are caves in cliffs on both sides of a valley which has a stream running through it. People lived in the caves at various times throughout the last Ice Age. Herds of animals used to come through the valley, and there were fish and waterfowl in the stream. Hundreds of flints and animal bones have been found in the caves, including an engraving of a horse's head on a bone.

Hunter~gatherers

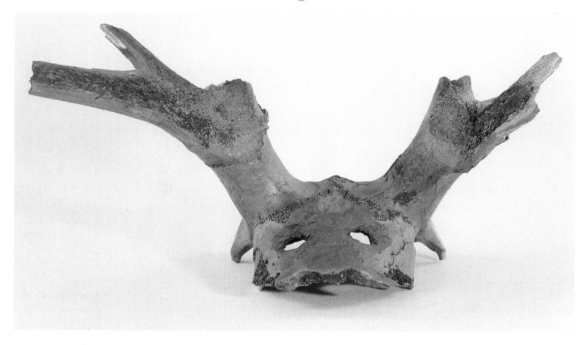

An antler head-dress from Starr Carr. Was it used for hunting or for a dance?

At the end of the last Ice Age, the weather became warmer, melting the ice sheets covering much of Britain. Small trees and bushes began to appear on the grasslands. They were followed by birch and pine woods, and finally by forests of oak, hazel, lime and elm trees. By 6000 BC the English Channel had formed and Britain became an island.

The surviving people from the last Ice Age were joined by hunter-fishermen from Scandinavia. They sailed over in small boats and began living by the edges of lakes and streams. One of their camps was found at Star Carr, in north Yorkshire.

It was built in 7500 BC. At the camp archaeologists have discovered a thick platform of saplings lying by what was once a lake. Several families had lived on this platform. The saplings for the platform had been chopped down with axes made of flint. The wet ground had preserved many pieces of bone, antler and wood, including harpoons, mattocks (a farming tool similar to a pick) and rolls of the bark of birch trees. A wooden paddle was found, which showed that the people used canoes. Several deer skulls, with their antlers, were also unearthed. These may have been used as disguises for deer

ABOVE Small, sharp flints were fixed into pieces of wood and used for hunting animals or harpooning fish.

hunting or, perhaps, for a dance to bring good luck to a hunting trip.

As the forests grew, new animals appeared, such as the wild pig, elk, ox and roe deer. Dogs were kept as pets, as well as for hunting. Many of the hunter-gatherer people used microliths. These were small, sharp flints which were either fixed to the end of lengths of wood as spear or arrow points, or slotted into wood and glued with resin to make harpoons or saws. Most people survived by gathering food – including nuts, berries, plants and shellfish.

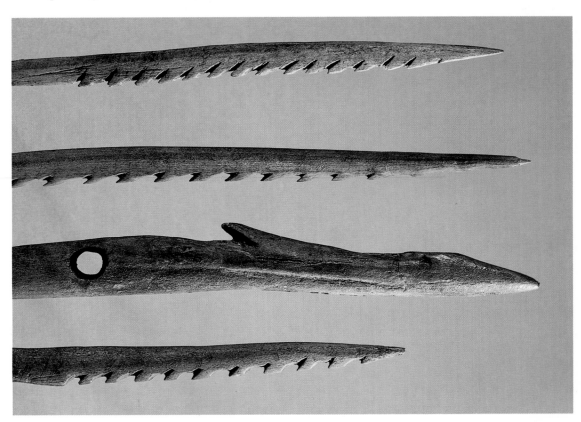

These pieces of antlers were sharpened and used for harpooning fish in rivers. The spiked edges stopped the fish slipping off after they had been caught.

The first farmers

ABOVE Pottery bowls, like this one, were made by the farmers in their spare time. They were used for storage and cooking.

Sometime around 4000 BC, at the start of the Neolithic Age, small groups began arriving in Britain from Europe. These people have been called the first farmers because they planted crops and kept herds of animals to supply them with food and clothing. The settlers seem to have lived peacefully with the other inhabitants of Britain. The farmers' new ways of producing food meant that, for the first time, people could live in one place all the time and not have to move about to find their food.

In southern England, the new farmers built villages with circular rings of ditches and banks. The banks had gaps in them for entrances, so archaeologists have called them 'causewayed camps'. A good example of one is Windmill Hill in Wiltshire. The banks were probably for keeping enemies out. The area in the middle of the rings seems to have been a place where tribes met and traded.

The settlers from Europe also brought the earliest pottery that we know about. To begin with, their pots were very rough and they had no decorations. They also had round bottoms. Later, they had flat bottoms and patterns made by animal bones, sticks or finger nails.

In western Britain, stone was dug out of the sides of mountains, such as Great Langdale in Cumbria, for trading. In eastern and southern England, flint was more easily available. Since the best flint was found deep in chalk soil, flint-mines had to be dug, like the one at Grimes Graves, in Norfolk. Here shafts up to 35 m deep were sunk into the ground. At the bottom of these shafts, low tunnels went in all directions along the layers of flint. Miners worked by the light of lamps. These were made out of a lump of chalk which had been hollowed out so that it could hold animal fat. A wick of made dried moss was dipped into this and lit. The miners used picks made from deer-antlers to dig the flint out.

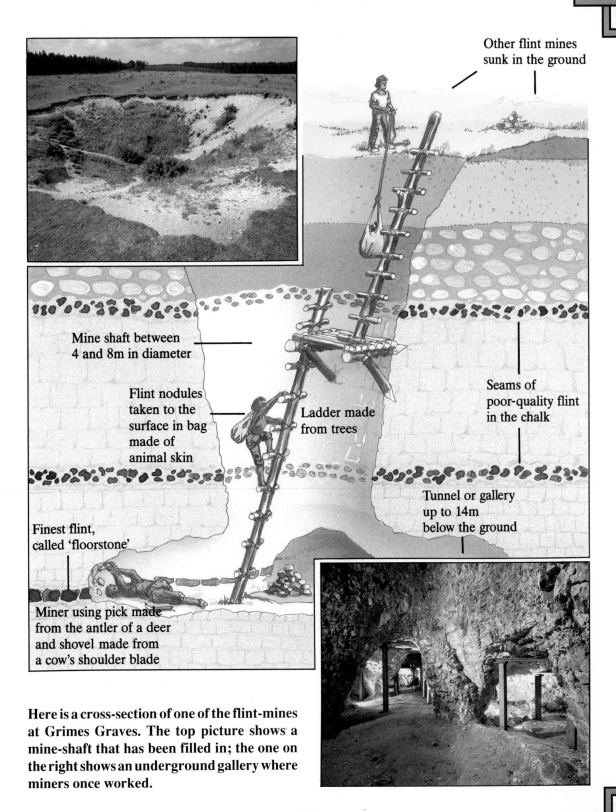

Other flint mines
sunk in the ground

Mine shaft between
4 and 8m in diameter

Flint nodules
taken to the
surface in bag
made of
animal skin

Ladder made
from trees

Seams of
poor-quality flint
in the chalk

Finest flint,
called 'floorstone'

Tunnel or gallery
up to 14m
below the ground

Miner using pick made
from the antler of a deer
and shovel made from
a cow's shoulder blade

Here is a cross-section of one of the flint-mines
at Grimes Graves. The top picture shows a
mine-shaft that has been filled in; the one on
the right shows an underground gallery where
miners once worked.

Tribal tombs

West Kennet long barrow in Wiltshire. The large stone blocking the entrance is 3.7 m high. Inside, there is a passage 12 m long, with small rooms either side.

The first farmers built large mounds of earth to bury important people. Most of these mounds were long banks, called long barrows, although some were round or oval in shape. Two ditches were dug alongside each other to provide the soil, and the barrow mound was raised between them. These barrows could be up to 100 m long, 12 m wide and 4 m high. One end, often the eastern one, was wider and higher than the other.

In the higher end, there were entrances to rooms inside the mound. The earliest barrows had wooden rooms inside them; later ones had stone passages with small rooms leading off to the right and left. The remains of the dead, perhaps chiefs or important members of a tribe, were put inside these rooms. The first farmers

ABOVE A round barrow at Bryn Celli Ddu, on Anglesey. It has a passage with one room at the end.

practised what we call collective burial, that is, placing the dead together and adding to them over the years.

Archaeologists now think that these burial places were not simply tombs, but shrines where ancestors were worshipped. They also think that remains, such as skulls or arm and leg bones, were taken by tribal priests for magical ceremonies to bring luck to the living. Offerings were laid at the entrances of these 'houses for the dead', including pots containing food and drink.

West Kennet, in Wiltshire, is one of the finest long barrows. The huge stones used to build the walls and roofs of the rooms can be seen today. When the barrow was excavated in the 1950s, the bones of 46 people were discovered.

In the long barrow at Stoney Littleton, Avon, dead people, along with some belongings, were put in small rooms like this one.

Temples and houses

After 3000 BC, causewayed camps were replaced by large circular enclosures, called henges. These consisted of high banks surrounding deep ditches, which enclosed a flat, central area. There were one or two entrances. Where there were two, they were usually opposite each other.

Archaeologists think that these large earthworks were meeting-places for the local tribes, where various activities took place. Some of these were religious. Often circles of tall, upright stones were raised round the inner edge of the ditch, with more stones at the centre, perhaps to show the risings and settings of the sun or moon at different times of the year. Sometimes these uprights were large wooden posts. Some henges, such as Durrington

The inside of one of the stone huts at Skara Brae, Mainland in Orkney. There were no trees on the island, so the furniture, walls and roofs were all made of stone. The village was buried under sand until 1851, when a storm blew most of it away, revealing the huts beneath it.

The henge at Avebury, in Wiltshire. Around the outside was a bank, which was separated by a ditch from the central area where the stones are. Perhaps people sat on the bank to watch ceremonies in the centre?

Walls and Marden in Wiltshire, contained wooden buildings with thatched roofs instead of circles of stones or posts.

Avebury in Wiltshire is the finest henge in Britain. It measured 465 m across with a bank 8 m high and a ditch 10 m deep. Huge stones, 98 in all, formed an outer circle, with two inner circles side by side. Parallel rows of stones formed avenues leading out of each of four entrances. Only one avenue has survived, the Kennet Avenue, which leads from the southern entrance.

Houses from Neolithic times are hard to find as most were wooden buildings which have left few remains. However, in the Orkneys, a group of stone-built huts can be seen at Skara Brae. They were protected by a thick sand covering until recent times. Inside you can see well-preserved remains, including fireplaces, cupboards, beds and shellfish tanks – all built of the local stone because there were no trees to use for wood.

The Bronze Age

Early Bronze Age pottery, such as this food vessel, was often beautifully decorated with very complicated patterns which had been pressed or scraped into the clay.

ABOVE A reconstruction of a Bronze Age dagger. Its handle is made of bone and joined to the blade with rivets.

After 2500 BC, many new ideas and ways of doing things came to Britain from Europe. We are not sure whether these were brought by trade or by new families of settlers, who archaeologists call the Beaker Folk. They got their name from a new type of pot which appeared at this time. The pots have been called beakers, and many had long necks. They were all a reddish colour and they were beautifully decorated with complicated designs. Beakers became popular throughout Britain. They were probably made by skilled potters for rich people.

Things made of metal also appeared in Britain for the first time. At first copper was used. Then people went on to use a mixture of copper and tin, called bronze. The earliest metal tools were simple and were made in open moulds. They included axes and daggers with flat blades, which often had neatly decorated wooden handles and bone pommels. Later, valuable jewellery and ornaments were made. Some of these were for the rich; others were produced for burial purposes – as were some of the best beakers.

These items were created by clever craftsmen, and included beads, buttons, rings and necklaces of jet, shale and amber. Bronze was sometimes used for bracelets and ear-rings, but the rarer and more beautiful pieces of jewellery were made from Irish gold.

This necklace was made of beads of polished jet (a type of coal). It was found in Scotland near Poltallock, Argyll.

Barrows and burials

About the year 2000 BC, at the start of the Bronze Age, there was a change in the way people were buried. Instead of burying many people in one tomb, dead people were placed on their own beneath small, circular mounds, called round barrows. Under these mounds, a person was laid, in a crouched position, in an oval grave, along with some grave-goods which his or her family and friends thought would be needed in the life-after-death. Men were often buried with hunting or military equipment – bows and arrows, archers' wristguards, daggers and axes. Women were buried with some jewellery, leather-working tools or small ornaments. Beakers, perhaps containing mead, often accompanied important persons. Rich

Some beakers had short necks; others had long necks, like this example found in a grave alongside a skeleton. It may have contained mead or some food.

people were buried with a lot of items, whereas some poor people often had nothing put in their graves. Many round barrows cover more than one grave. This shows that the area was often left open for some time before the earth was piled on top of the graves to form a mound.

In southern Britain, mounds were generally built of soil or turf. In the north, they were often made of cairns of stones, with the bodies lying in graves cut out of

ABOVE The remains of a cairn of stones near Inverness in Scotland.

The Devil's Arrows at Boroughbridge, North Yorkshire: three tall stones standing on their own in a long line.

the rock or in boxes of stone slabs, called cists. Barrows were often arranged in cemeteries, like the one at Oakley Down, in Dorset, which got bigger over the centuries.

Other landmarks also remind us of the religious ceremonies of Bronze Age people. There are many stone circles and tall stones, standing on their own, called monoliths, like the three Devil's Arrows at Boroughbridge, in North Yorkshire. Rocks carved with 'cup-and-ring' marks, which are mainly found in northern Britain, are also thought by archaeologists to be connected with religion.

Stonehenge

Stonehenge is the most famous prehistoric site in Europe. It was built before 3000 BC as a henge with one entrance, with a ditch surrounded by a bank. A monolith, the Heel Stone, stood outside the entrance, and there were probably four station stones inside the bank.

One thousand years later, a stone circle was put up at its centre. The stones for the circle were brought all the way from the Preseli Mountains in South Wales. A ditch-and-bank avenue was also dug, leading from the entrance. This was positioned so that it would line up with the sunrise on Midsummer's Day.

ABOVE The tops of Stonehenge's upright stones were designed to fit into holes in the lintel stones put across them.

Around 2100 BC the stone circle was knocked down and a vast new temple was built in its place. Huge stones were dragged from the Marlborough Downs, 38 km away, shaped and trimmed, and set up in a ring, 30 m round. The upright stones had a continuous circle of lintels laid on top of them. The lintels were made very carefully, so that they fitted exactly. Inside the ring there were five massive stones, called trilithons. These were higher

'Long Meg and Her Daughters', which is the name of a circle of stones at Little Salked, near Penrith, in Cumbria.

Stonehenge has a circle of stones within a henge. It probably had several functions: a meeting-place, a place for trading goods and a temple for religious ceremonies.

than the outer circle, and they were arranged in a horseshoe. The tall Altar Stone stood in front of the south-western trilithon. On Midsummer's Day, the sun rose directly over the Heel Stone and its rays shone on to the Altar Stone through a gap in the outer circle. Later, another circle of the Welsh stones was built inside the outer ring of stones, and more were arranged in a horseshoe inside the trilithons. Stonehenge was completed around 1500 BC. Today it reminds us of how clever the Bronze Age people of Salisbury Plain must have been.

Iron Age farmers

About 800 BC, traders from Europe began bringing a new metal to Britain – iron. For this reason, we call the period after the Bronze Age, the Iron Age. Life in Britain continued much as before, but the new iron tools made it much easier to chop down the forests and clear the land for farming. The earth could now be turned over with a new type of plough, which was pulled by two oxen. Land for growing crops was divided into small, rectangular fields. Farming remained the main way of life, and most of the farms were small, as the remains at Little Woodbury (Wiltshire), Staple Howe (east Yorkshire) and Grimspound (Devon) show us.

Families lived in round huts with thatched roofs. The walls were built of stone, or woven branches (called wattle) covered with clay (called daub). In the lowlands of the south, wheat and barley were grown and animals herded. In the highlands of the north and west, where the soil was not so good for growing

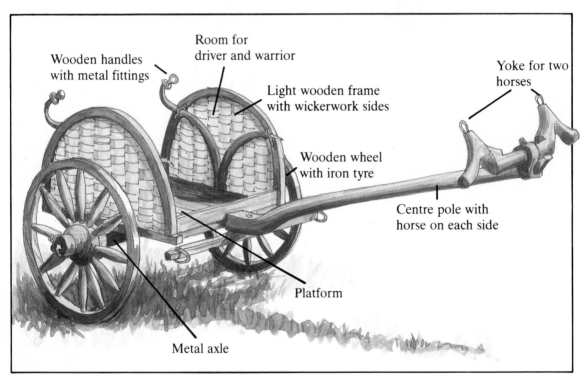

Wooden handles with metal fittings

Room for driver and warrior

Light wooden frame with wickerwork sides

Yoke for two horses

Wooden wheel with iron tyre

Centre pole with horse on each side

Platform

Metal axle

This Iron Age chariot would have been pulled into battle by two horses. It was light and fast and had room for a driver and a warrior.

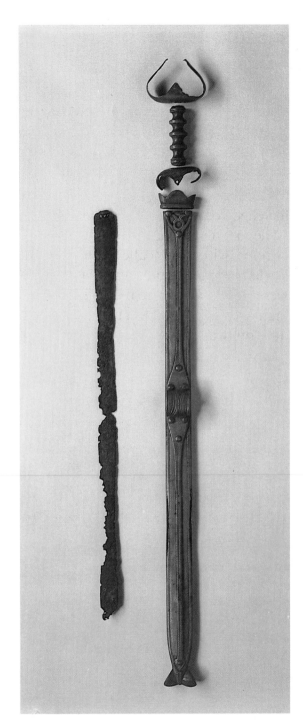

The blade, handle and scabbard of a sword, found at Cotterdale, Yorkshire.

ABOVE These are the remains of a farm at Grimspound, in Devon.

crops, farmers mainly bred cattle, sheep and pigs. In the south, the wheat and barley were dried and stored in deep chalk pits for eating in winter. Many pits became 'dustbins' into which all sorts of rubbish was thrown. Archaeologists can sift through this material to build up an interesting picture of daily life.

Wheat was turned into flour by crushing it between the stones of a quern, and then baked into flat cakes. Pots were very rough, but many wooden dishes, bowls and beakers, produced on lathes, were used. Most of these have rotted away in the soil. However, archaeologists have found stone weights from looms and combs made of bone, which show that cloth was woven, probably in chequered patterns. It was coloured with dyes made from berries.

Hillforts

Many large Iron Age groups became very powerful, with their chiefs ruling over many other groups. The more powerful chiefs began building small hillforts to protect their people in time of war with neighbouring tribes.

The earliest hillforts had a single rampart with a high wooden fence on top. A deep ditch was dug around the rampart.

After 500 BC, the biggest tribes built larger hillforts. Many of these had two or three ramparts and ditches, and carefully designed entrances which were difficult to attack. Although many of these forts were on hills, some were built on low ground. These had extra tall ramparts and very deep ditches to protect them.

Many of these larger hillforts became

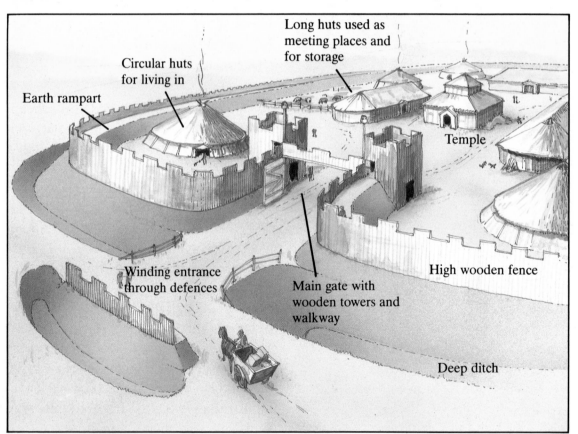

A lot of timber was required to build an Iron Age hillfort, most of it for the high fences that surrounded it. As a result, many forests were destroyed for ever.

The three rows of banks and ditches and the well-protected entrances of the hillforts at Maiden Castle, in Dorset, can still be seen.

the headquarters of tribes. The hillforts were surrounded by farming land where most of the tribespeople lived and worked. In times of trouble, they could shelter in the fort. Perhaps the finest and best-preserved hillfort is Maiden Castle, in Dorset. Its three rows of banks and ditches and two well-protected entrances can still be seen.

Another important hillfort is at Danebury in Hampshire. Archaeologists have done a lot of excavating here and found out much about it. They have discovered that Danebury was really a small town, where some 300 to 500 people lived. Many storage pits show that barley and wheat, and other crops, were brought there from the surrounding farms. There were also temples and workshops, as well as the homes of the chief and his family.

Archaeologists know that there were about 1,400 hillforts in England and Wales alone. Finding the wood to build them led to many of the forests being cut down.

Tribes

A huge horse carved in the chalky hillside near Uffington, in Oxfordshire. Archaeologists think that it was probably made by the Atrebates tribe to show that they ruled the area.

It is only in the later years of the Iron Age that we learn of the names of individual tribes and the regions they occupied. Around 250 BC, a people called the Marnians came from Europe. One Marnian tribe, known as the Parisi, settled in east Yorkshire and began burying their dead in barrows again. Their chiefs were sometimes buried with two-wheeled chariots which had been taken to bits, and

ABOVE This Iron Age helmet was found at the bottom of the River Thames at Waterloo Bridge in London.

cremated their dead, and often buried their ashes in urns or bronze buckets, sometimes along with a few precious grave-goods.

The Celts worshipped a number of gods. The god called Cernunnos seems to have been the most important. The Celts believed that their gods lived in rivers, wells and streams, or in rocks and woods. Their priests were the Druids, who were very powerful and carried out the human sacrifices which were part of their religion. The Druids were eventually wiped out by the Romans in AD 43.

often many expensive grave-goods. One of their cemeteries, the Danes Graves, near Driffield, originally contained some 500 barrows.

After 100 BC, groups of tribes, collectively known as the Belgae, moved across the Channel into south-east England. They included the Catuvellauni, the Regni and the Atrebates. They fought among themselves, as well as conquering other tribes to their west and north, and gradually extending their territory. The Belgae were superb metal craftsmen who produced a variety of fine products, both for decoration and for use in battle. They introduced the first coins, which were copies of Greek ones. They also brought the potter's wheel to Britain, and traded with the Romans. A wide range of Roman goods was transported to the big markets which they set up, such as the ones near to Colchester and St Albans. They

ABOVE This beautiful shield was made by a craftsman from a Belgic tribe. It was found at Battersea, in London.

Finding lost sites

Nowadays archaeologists have many methods which enable them to find lost sites and reconstruct the past by experiments. One important way of doing this is aerial photography. Remains of sites, destroyed long ago, can still be seen from the air. Growing crops can reveal buried walls and ditches and their shapes, because crops do not grow the same in the soil over a buried wall or over a ditch. These cropmarks, as they are called, can be seen from a plane.

Ploughed fields often show 'soil marks'. Ploughed-up barrows and banks often appear clearly because of the different soil colours which are brought to the surface. Shallow ditches and low banks, scarcely visible on the ground, can be seen as 'shadow sites' in the early morning or evening by the longer shadows thrown by the low angle of a rising or setting sun.

Iron Age people probably lived in huts like this one on the farm at Butser, in Hampshire.

Experimental Archaeology is a new way of reconstructing the past. At Butser Iron Age Farm, in Hampshire, a complete, working prehistoric farm has been built, including roundhouses, animals bred from species very like late prehistoric ones, and crops grown in the Iron Age way from types of grain common then. The seeds are sown and harvested using ancient methods, in fields prepared by a plough pulled by two oxen. Other experiments include threshing and drying the grain, and storing it in pits. They are even trying to grow some Iron Age weeds, many of which were either eaten or used as herbs or medicines.

ABOVE Iron Age farmers made shelters to protect their straw. BELOW They would have used a plough like this in their fields.

Places to visit

Arbor Low henge, Middleton, Derbyshire

Avebury henge, Wiltshire

Butser Iron Age Farm Project, Queen Elizabeth Country Park, Hampshire

Castell Henllys Iron Age settlement, Nevern, Dyfed

Castlerigg stone circle, Keswick, Cumbria

Creswell Crags caves, Whitwell, Derbyshire

Devil's Arrows standing stones, Boroughbridge, North Yorkshire

Duggleby Howe barrow, Kirby Grindalythe, East Yorkshire

Flag Fen Bronze Age settlement, Peterborough, Northamptonshire

Grimes Graves flint mines, near Thetford, Norfolk

Ilkley Moor carved stone and circles, West Yorkshire

Maes Howe barrow, Mainland, Orkney

Maiden Castle hillfort, Winterborne St Martin, Dorset

Oakley Down barrow group, Wimborne St Giles, Dorset

Rudston standing stones, East Yorkshire

Silbury Hill giant mound, Avebury, Wiltshire

Skara Brae village, Mainland, Orkney

Stanton Moor barrow cemetery and circles, Birchover, Derbyshire

Stonehenge, Amesbury, Wiltshire

West Kennet long barrow, Wiltshire

Winterborne Stoke barrow group, Wiltshire

Museums

Ashmolean Museum, Oxford

British Museum, London

Devizes Museum, Wiltshire

Dorchester Museum, Dorset

Hull Museum, Humberside

Salisbury Museum, Wiltshire

Sheffield Museum, South Yorkshire

Young Archaeologists Club

If you are interested in finding out more about archaeology, you might like to join this club. Further information can be obtained from: Young Archaeologists Club, United House, Piccadilly, York YO1 1PQ.

Books to read

Dyer, J. *Your Book of Prehistoric Britain* (Faber, 1974)

Jamieson, J. M. *Britain in the Stone and Iron Ages* (Arnold, 1979)

Nichol, J. *Evidence in History – Prehistoric Britain* (Blackwell, 1983)

Reynolds, P. J. *Farming in the Iron Age* (Cambridge, 1976)

Sauvain, P. A. *Prehistoric Britain* (Macmillan, 1976)

Triggs, T. D. *Ancient Britons* (Oliver & Boyd, 1981)

Glossary

Amber A hard, clear yellowish substance which was used for making things like beads, necklaces and buttons in the Early Bronze Age.

Avenue A path leading from henge entrances or smaller stone circles. They are marked by rows of standing stones or ditches and banks.

Barrow A mound of earth, either long (long barrow) or circular (round barrow), which was put on top of important dead people in prehistoric times.

Beaker A tall, well-made pottery container brought to Britain in the late part of the Neolithic period.

Bronze A metal made from copper and tin.

Bronze Age The years when tools and weapons were made of bronze.

Cairn A burial mound made of stones.

Causewayed camps The earliest Neolithic earthworks. They are found in southern England and made of rings of banks and ditches which contain gaps (the causeways) in them.

Celts A group of people who lived in western Europe in the Iron Age. Some Celtic tribes moved to Britain during this period.

Cist A box of stones, usually with a covering slab, found underneath a round cairn and used for the burial of one person in the Bronze Age.

Earthwork Any structure built of earth, for example, a barrow or hillfort.

Grave-goods Anything left in a grave for a person to use in the life-after-death.

Henge A Neolithic earthwork with an outer bank, inner ditch and one or two entrances. It often contained a stone circle.

Hillfort An Iron Age village, protected by banks and ditches.

Homo sapiens Humans who looked like us, who first appeared in Europe about 40,000 BC, during the last Ice Age.

Jet A type of black coal which can be polished. It was used to make ornaments in the Early Bronze Age.

Megalithic Built of large stones.

Microliths Very small flints, used as points, blades or tools in the Mesolithic years.

Monolith A single tall standing stone.

Mesolithic The Middle Stone Age (10,000–4,300 BC).

Neolithic The New Stone Age (4300–2000 BC).

Palaeolithic The Old Stone Age, the earliest period of human life on earth (any time before 10,000 BC).

Quern A hand-mill for grinding corn.

Rampart A bank of earth and stones, usually to protect a village or a fort.

Shale A kind of rock used for making things like rings and beads in the Early Bronze Age.

Urn A type of pot dating from the Early Bronze Age. It was used for liquids or food, or for holding the ashes of the dead.

Index